Wood Pellet Smoker Cookbook 2021

A Complete Beginners Guide To Traeger Grill Bible To Smoking And Grilling Flavorful And Tasty Recipes

Written By

MICHAEL BLACKWOOD

© Copyright 2021 - All rights reserved.

The content contained within this book may not be reproduced, duplicated or transmitted without direct written permission from the author or the publisher.

Under no circumstances will any blame or legal responsibility be held against the publisher, or author, for any damages, reparation, or monetary loss due to the information contained within this book. Either directly or indirectly.

Legal Notice:

This book is copyright protected. This book is only for personal use. You cannot amend, distribute, sell, use, quote or paraphrase any part, or the content within this book, without the consent of the author or publisher.

Disclaimer Notice:

Please note the information contained within this document is for educational and entertainment purposes only. All effort has been executed to present accurate, up to date, and reliable, complete information. No warranties of any kind are declared or implied. Readers acknowledge that the author is not engaging in the rendering of legal, financial, medical or professional advice. The content within this book has been derived from various sources. Please consult a licensed professional before attempting any techniques outlined in this book.

By reading this document, the reader agrees that under no circumstances is the author responsible for any losses, direct or indirect, which are incurred as a result of the use of information contained within this document, including, but not limited to, — errors, omissions, or inaccuracies.

Table of Contents

- PART 1 - 9

WOOD PELLET SMOKER COOKBOOK 9

BARBECUE 11

    Barbecue Steak 12

APPETIZERS AND SIDES 15

    Grilled Broccoli 16

    Smoked Coleslaw 17

    The Best Potato Roast 19

BEEF 21

    Lemony Mustard Crusted Veal 22

    Classic Burger 24

    Green Burgers 26

    Stuffed Peppers 28

LAMB 31

    Leg of Lamb 32

    Smoked Lamb chops 34

    Wood Pellet Smoked Lamb Shoulder 36

CHICKEN 39

    Bacon Cordon Blue 40

    Lemon Cornish Chicken Stuffed With Crab 42

    Pellet Smoked Chicken Burgers 44

    Perfect Smoked Chicken Patties 46

TURKEY 49

- Spatchcock Smoked Turkey _____ 50
- Hoisin Turkey Wings _____ 52

PORK _____ 55
- Pork Butt _____ 56
- Pineapple Bourbon Glazed Ham _____ 58
- Pork Tacos _____ 60
- Cider Pork Steak _____ 62
- Raspberry Chipotle Pork Kebabs _____ 64
- Bacon Cheese Fries _____ 66
- Candied Bacon _____ 68
- Bacon Wrapped Onion Rings _____ 70
- Braised Pork Carnitas _____ 72
- Cuban Pork _____ 74

DESSERT _____ 77
- Bread Pudding _____ 78
- Smoked Chocolate Bacon Pecan Pie _____ 81

RUBS, SAUCES, MARINADES, AND GLAZES _____ 84
- Smokey Beef Rib Rub _____ 85
- Hellfire Cajun Rub _____ 86
- Carolina Basting Mop _____ 87
- Basic Vinegar Mop _____ 88

- PART 2 - _____ 89

ELECTRIC SMOKER COOKBOOK _____ 89

APPETIZERS, VEGETABLES, AND SIDES _____ 91
- Smoked Potato Salad _____ 92
- Smoked Volcano Potatoes _____ 94

Groovy smoked asparagus	96
BEEF	**99**
Meaty Chuck Short Ribs	100
Smoked Pete-zza Meatloaf	102
Smoked Tenderloin Teriyaki	104
LAMB	**107**
Spicy Brown Smoked Lamb Ribs	108
CHICKEN	**112**
Smoked Paprika Chicken	113
Fully Smoked Herbal Chicken	115
Orange Crispy Chicken	117
TURKEY	**121**
Turkey in the Electric Smoker	122
PORK	**125**
Smoked Pork Loin with Sweet Habanero Rub	126
Smoked Pork Ribs with Avocado Oil	128
Smoked Pork Ribs with Fresh Herbs	130
SEAFOOD	**132**
Smoked Tuna	133
Smoked Snapper Fillet	135
Delicious Trout Fillets	137
RUBS, SAUCES, MARINADES, AND GLAZES	**139**
6-Ingredient Turkey Brine	140
Brine for Fish	142

- PART 1 -

WOOD PELLET SMOKER COOKBOOK

The Wood Pellet Smoke and Grill is a durable and cost-effective option for anyone who wants to smoke or grill without worrying all the time. Because of its quality of construction, it works effectively for a long time. You only need to spend a few minutes after cooking to maintain its cleanliness. This keeps the fuel efficiency high and allows for controlled wood pellet burning. Thus, you get a perfect temperature for the type of cooking approach you are following. The rate of pellet burning increases when you are grilling, and it decreases when you set the smoker-grill at a low temperature. This helps to smoke your food for a long time with a consistent heat.

BARBECUE

Barbecue Steak

Preparation Time: 5 minutes
Cooking Time: 45 minutes
Servings: 4

Ingredients:

- 2 bone-in rib eye steaks
- Steak seasoning
- 1 cup barbecue sauce

Directions:

1. Sprinkle both sides of the steak with the rub.
2. Turn on the wood pellet grill.
3. Set it to 400 degrees F.

4. Grill it for 7 to 8 minutes per side.
5. Transfer the steaks to a cutting board.
6. Let sit for 10 minutes before slicing.
7. Using a pan over medium heat, simmer the barbecue sauce for 5 minutes.
8. Serve the grilled steak with the barbecue sauce.

Nutrition: Calories: 330 Carbs: 47g

Fat: 6g Protein: 20g

APPETIZERS AND SIDES

Grilled Broccoli

Preparation Time: 15 minutes

Cooking Time: 10 minutes

Servings: 4 to 6

Ingredients:

- 4 bunches of Broccoli
- 4 tablespoons Olive oil
- Black pepper and salt to taste
- ½ Lemon, the juice
- ½ Lemon cut into wedges

Directions:

1. Preheat the grill to High with closed lid.
2. In a bowl add the broccoli and drizzle with oil. Coat well. Season with salt.
3. Grill for 5 minutes and then flip. Cook for 3 minutes more.
4. Once done transfer on a plate. Squeeze lemon on top and serve with lemon wedges. Enjoy!

Smoked Coleslaw

Preparation Time: 15 minutes

Cooking Time: 25 minutes

Servings: 8

Ingredients:

- 1 shredded Purple Cabbage
- 1 shredded Green Cabbage
- 2 Scallions, sliced
- 1 cup Carrots, shredded
- Dressing
- 1 tablespoon of Celery Seed
- 1/8 cup of White vinegar
- 1 ½ cups Mayo

- Black pepper and salt to taste

Directions:

1. Preheat the grill to 180F with closed lid.
2. On a tray spread the carrots and cabbage. Place the tray on the grate and smoke for about 25 minutes.
3. Transfer in the fridge to cool.
4. In the meantime make the dressing. In a bowl combine the ingredients. Mix well.
5. Transfer the veggies in a bowl. Drizzle with the sauce and toss
6. Serve sprinkled with scallions.

Nutrition: Calories: 35g Protein: 1g Carbs: 5g Fat: 5g

The Best Potato Roast

Preparation Time: 15 minutes

Cooking Time: 35 minutes

Servings: 6

Ingredients:

- 4 Potatoes, large (scrubbed)
- 1 ½ cups gravy (beef or chicken)
- Rib seasoning to taste
- 1 ½ cups Cheddar cheese
- Black pepper and salt to taste
- 2 tablespoons sliced Scallions

Directions:

1. Preheat the grill to high with closed lid.
2. Slice each potato into wedges or fries. Transfer into a bowl and drizzle with oil. Season with Rib seasoning.
3. Spread the wedges/fries on a baking sheet (rimmed). Roast for about 20 minutes. Turn the wedges/fries and cook for 15 minutes more.
4. In the meantime in a saucepan warm the chicken/beef gravy. Cut the cheese into small cubes.
5. Once done cooking place the potatoes on a plate or into a bowl. Distribute the cut cheese and pour hot gravy on top.
6. Serve garnished with scallion. Season with pepper. Enjoy!

Nutrition: Calories: 220 Protein: 3g Carbs: 38g Fat: 15g

BEEF

Lemony Mustard Crusted Veal

Preparation Time: 10 minutes

Cooking Time: 2 hours 30 minutes

Servings: 2

Ingredients:

- Pepper
- Salt
- ¼ cup breadcrumbs
- 2 tablespoons water
- 1 teaspoon basil
- 1 pound veal round roast
- 1 tablespoon Dijon mustard
- 1 tablespoon lemon juice

Directions:

1. Lay the roast in a shallow roasting pan on a rack.
2. Mix together the pepper, thyme, basil, lemon juice, mustard, water, and breadcrumbs.
3. Spread this mixture over the roast being sure to get all sides.
4. Add wood pellets to your smoker and follow your cooker's startup procedure. Preheat your smoker, with your lid closed, until it reaches 450.

5. Place the roast onto the grill and cook for ten minutes per side until it is to your desired doneness.
6. Take off from the grill and allow to set for ten minutes.

Nutrition: Calories: 390 Carbs: 0g Fat: 15g Protein: 40g

Classic Burger

Preparation Time: 10 minutes

Cooking Time: 1 hour

Servings: 6

Ingredients:

- Pepper
- Salt
- 1 chopped onion
- ½ pound ground pork
- 1 tablespoon chopped parsley
- 4 tablespoon olive oil
- 1 ¼ pounds ground beef

- Toppings of choice

Directions:

1. Combine all together all of the ingredients, except the toppings.
2. Use your hands and mix the ingredients well until everything is thoroughly combined. Form into six patties.
3. Place into the refrigerator for 30 minutes.
4. Add wood pellets to your smoker and follow your cooker's startup procedure. Preheat your smoker, with your lid closed, until it reaches 425.
5. Grill the burgers, covered, for four minutes on each side.
6. Serve with toppings of your choice.

Nutrition: Calories: 237 Carbs: 27g Fat: 9g Protein: 11g

Green Burgers

Preparation Time: 10 minutes
Cooking Time: 35 minutes
Servings: 4

Ingredients:

- Pepper
- 2 pounds ground beef
- 1 tablespoon chopped cilantro
- 1 egg
- 1 pound frozen spinach, thawed and drained
- 3 cloves garlic
- 3 tablespoons olive oil
- 1 tablespoon chopped tarragon
- Salt
- 2 chopped green onions

Directions:

1. Wash and chop the green onion. Mix the onion and spinach together.
2. Add in the salt, pepper, cilantro, tarragon, oil, egg, garlic, and ground beef.
3. Use your two hands and mix all the ingredients until everything is thoroughly combined. Shape into six burgers.

4. Add wood pellets to your smoker and follow your cooker's startup procedure. Preheat your smoker, with your lid closed, until it reaches 380.
5. Cover the burgers after placing on the grill. Both sides should be cooked for 5 minutes.
6. Serve with toppings of choice.

Nutrition: Calories: 190 Carbs: 3g Fat: 10g Protein: 21g

Stuffed Peppers

Preparation Time: 10 minutes

Cooking Time: 2 hours

Servings: 4

Ingredients:

- 1 tablespoons garlic, minced
- 1 large diced onion
- 1 ½ cup grated cheddar, divided
- 1 teaspoon pepper
- 14 ounces can tomato paste
- 1 teaspoon seasoned salt
- ½ pound sausage
- ½ pound ground beef
- 1 poblano chili, seeded and chopped
- 4 large bell peppers, seeds, top, and core removed

Directions:

1. Lay the peppers inside of a disposable aluminum pan. If they won't stay upright on their own, you can wrap a foil ring around their base to keep them standing.
2. Add wood pellets to your smoker and follow your cooker's startup procedure. Preheat your smoker, with your lid closed, until it reaches 350.

3. Using the stovetop, heat a large pan. Brown the sausage and the beef for five to seven minutes. Drain the fat and crumble up the meat.
4. Mix in the garlic, pepper, and salt, cup of cheese, tomato paste, poblano, and onion. Stir until everything is well combined.
5. Place the meat mixture in the peppers. Put the pan onto the grill, cover, and let them smoke for an hour.
6. Top the peppers with the remaining cheese and allow them to smoke, covered, for another 15 minutes. Serve.

Nutrition: Calories: 243 Carbs: 28g Fat: 7g Protein: 19g

LAMB

Leg of Lamb

Preparation Time: 10 minutes
Cooking Time: 2 hours
Servings: 6

Ingredients:
- 1 (2 pounds) leg of lamb
- 1 teaspoon dried rosemary
- 2 teaspoon freshly ground black pepper
- 4 cloves garlic (minced)
- 2 teaspoon salt or more to taste
- ½ teaspoon paprika
- 1 teaspoon thyme
- 2 tablespoons olive oil
- 1 teaspoon brown sugar
- 2 tablespoons oregano

Directions:
1. Trim the meat of excess fat and remove silver-skin.
2. In a mixing bowl, combine the thyme, salt, sugar, oregano, paprika, black pepper, garlic and olive oil.
3. Generously, rub the mixture over the leg of lamb. Cover seasoned leg of lamb with foil and let it sit for 1 hour to marinate.

4. Start your grill on smoke and leave the lid open for 5 minutes, or until fire starts. Cover the lid and preheat grill to 250°F using hickory, maple or apple wood pellets.
5. Remove the foil and place the leg of lamb on a smoker rack. Place the rack on the grill and smoke the leg of lamb for about 4 hours, or until it reach the internal temperature of your meat 145°F. Take off the leg of lamb from the grill and let it rest for a few minutes to cool. Cut into sizes and serve.

Nutrition: Calories 334 Fat: 16g Carbs: 2.9g Protein 42.9g

Smoked Lamb chops

Preparation Time: 10 Minutes
Cooking Time: 50 Minutes
Servings: 4

Ingredients:
- 1 rack of lamb, fat trimmed
- 2 tablespoons rosemary, fresh
- 2 tablespoons sage, fresh
- 1 tablespoon garlic cloves, roughly chopped
- 1/2 tablespoon salt
- 1/2 tablespoon pepper, coarsely ground
- 1/4 cup olive oil
- 1 tablespoon honey

Directions:
1. Preheat your wood pellet smoker to 225°F using a fruitwood.
2. Put all your ingredients except the lamb in a food processor. Liberally apply the mixture on the lamb.
3. Place the lamb on the smoker for 45 minutes or until the internal temperature reaches 120°F.
4. Sear the lamb on the grill for 2 minutes per side. Let rest for 5 minutes before serving. Slice and enjoy.

Nutrition: Calories 704 Fat 56g Carbs 24g Protein 27g

Wood Pellet Smoked Lamb Shoulder

Preparation Time: 10 Minutes
Cooking Time: 1hour 30 Minutes
Servings: 7

Ingredients:
- For Smoked Lamb Shoulder
- 5 pound lamb shoulder, boneless and excess fat trimmed
- 2 tablespoons kosher salt
- 2 tablespoons black pepper
- 1 tablespoon rosemary, dried
- The Injection
- 1 cup apple cider vinegar
- The Spritz
- 1 cup apple cider vinegar
- 1 cup apple juice

Directions:
1. Preheat the wood pellet smoker with a water pan to 2250 F.
2. Rinse the lamb in cold water then pat it dry with a paper towel. Inject vinegar to the lamb.

3. Pat the lamb dry again and rub with oil, salt black pepper and rosemary. Tie with kitchen twine.
4. Smoke uncovered for 1 hour then spritz after every 15 minutes until the internal temperature reaches 1950 F.
5. Take off the lamb from the grill and place it on a platter. Let cool before shredding it and enjoying it with your favorite side.

Nutrition: Calories 243 Fat 19g Carbs 0g Protein 17g

CHICKEN

Bacon Cordon Blue

Preparation Time: 30 Minutes
Cooking Time: 2 To 2.5 Hours
Servings: 6

Ingredients:

- 24 bacon slices
- 3 large boneless, skinless chicken breasts, butterfly
- 3 extra virgin olive oils with roasted garlic flavor
- 3 Yang original dry lab or poultry seasonings
- 12 slice black forest ham
- 12-slice provolone cheese

Directions:

1. Weave 4 slices of bacon tightly, leaving extra space on the edges. Bacon weave is used to interlock alternating bacon slices and wrap chicken cordon blue.
2. Slice or rub two chicken breast fillets with olive oil on both sides.
3. Scattered the seasoning mixture on both sides of the chicken breast.
4. Lay the seasoned chicken fillets on the bacon weave and slice one ham and one provolone cheese on each.

5. Repeat this process with another chicken fillet, ham and cheese. Fold chicken, ham and cheese in half.
6. Lay the bacon strips from the opposite corner to completely cover the chicken cordon blue.
7. Use a silicon food grade cooking band, butcher twine, and toothpick to secure the bacon strip in place.
8. Repeat this process for the remaining chicken breast and ingredients.
9. Using apple or cherry pellets, configure a wood pellet smoker grill for indirect cooking and preheat (180 ° F to 200 ° F) for smoking.
10. Inhale bacon cordon blue for 1 hour.
11. After smoking for 1 hour, raise the pit temperature to 350 ° F.
12. Bacon cordon blue occurs when the internal temperature reaches 165 ° F and the bacon becomes crispy.
13. Rest for 15 minutes under a loose foil tent before serving.

Nutrition: Calories: 250 Carbs: 11g Fat: 7g Protein: 34g

Lemon Cornish Chicken Stuffed With Crab

Preparation Time: 30 Minutes
Cooking Time: 1 Hour 30 Minutes
Servings: 4

Ingredients:

- 2 Cornish chickens (about 1¾ pound each)
- Half lemon, half
- 4 tablespoons western rub or poultry rub
- 2 cups stuffed with crab meat

Directions:

1. Rinse chicken thoroughly inside and outside, tap lightly and let it dry.
2. Carefully loosen the skin on the chest and legs. Rub the lemon under and over the skin and into the cavity. Rub the western lab under and over the skin on the chest and legs. Carefully return the skin to its original position.
3. Wrap the Cornish hen in plastic wrap and refrigerate for 2-3 hours until flavor is absorbed.
4. Prepare crab meat stuffing according to the instructions. Make sure it is completely cooled before packing the

chicken. Loosely fill the cavities of each hen with crab filling.
5. Tie the Cornish chicken legs with a butcher's leash to put the filling.
6. Set wood pellet smoker grill for indirect cooking and preheat to 375 ° F with pellets.
7. Place the stuffed animal on the rack in the baking dish. If you do not have a rack that is small enough to fit, you can also place the chicken directly on the baking dish.
8. Roast the chicken at 375 ° F until the inside temperature of the thickest part of the chicken breast reaches 170 ° F, the thigh reaches 180 ° F, and the juice is clear.
9. Test the crab meat stuffing to see if the temperature has reached 165 ° F.
10. Place the roasted chicken under a loose foil tent for 15 minutes before serving.

Nutrition: Calories: 275 Carbs: 0g Fat: 3g Protein: 32g

Pellet Smoked Chicken Burgers

Preparation Time: 15 minutes
Cooking Time: 1 hour 10 minutes
Servings: 6

Ingredients:
- 2 pounds ground chicken breast
- 2/3 cup of finely chopped onions
- 1 tablespoon of cilantro, finely chopped
- 2 tablespoons fresh parsley, finely chopped
- 2 tablespoons of olive oil
- 1/2 teaspoon of ground cumin
- 2 tablespoons of lemon juice freshly squeezed
- 3/4 teaspoon of salt and red pepper to taste

Directions:

1. In a bowl add all ingredients; mix until combined well.
2. Form the mixture into 6 patties.
3. Start your pellet grill on SMOKE (oak or apple pellets) with the lid open until the fire is established. Set the temperature to 350°F and preheat, lid closed, for 10 to 15 minutes.
4. Smoke the chicken burgers for 45 - 50 minutes or until cooked through, turning every 15 minutes.
5. Your burgers are ready when internal temperature reaches 165 °F. Serve hot.

Nutrition: Calories: 221 Carbs: 2.12g Fat: 8.5g Protein: 32.5g

Perfect Smoked Chicken Patties

Preparation Time: 15 minutes
Cooking Time: 55 minutes
Servings: 6

Ingredients:
- 2 pounds ground chicken breast
- 2/3 cup minced onion
- 1 Tablespoon cilantro (chopped)
- 2 Tablespoons fresh parsley, finely chopped
- 2 Tablespoons olive oil
- 1/8 teaspoon crushed red pepper powdered for the taste
- 1/2 teaspoon ground cumin
- 2 Tablespoons fresh lemon juice
- 3/4 teaspoon kosher salt
- 2 teaspoons paprika
- Hamburger buns for serving

Directions:
1. In a bowl combine all ingredients from the list.
2. Using your hands, mix well. Form mixture into 6 patties. Refrigerate until ready to grill (about 30 minutes).

3. Start your pellet grill on SMOKE with the lid open until the fire is established). Set the temperature to 350°F and preheat, lid closed, for 10 to 15 minutes.
4. Arrange chicken patties on the grill rack and cook for 35 to 40 minutes turning once.
5. Serve hot with hamburger buns and your favorite condiments.

Nutrition: Calories: 258 Carbs: 2.5g Fat: 9.4g Protein: 39g

TURKEY

Spatchcock Smoked Turkey

Preparation Time: 15 minutes
Cooking Time: 4 hours 3 minutes
Servings: 6

Ingredients:

- 1 (18 pounds) turkey
- 2 tablespoons finely chopped fresh parsley
- 1 tablespoon finely chopped fresh rosemary
- 2 tablespoons finely chopped fresh thyme
- ½ cup melted butter
- 1 teaspoon garlic powder
- 1 teaspoon onion powder
- 1 teaspoon ground black pepper
- 2 teaspoons salt or to taste
- 2 tablespoons finely chopped scallions

Directions:

1. Remove the turkey giblets and rinse turkey, in and out, under cold running water.
2. Place the turkey on a working surface, breast side down. Use a poultry shear to cut the turkey along both sides of the backbone to remove the turkey back bone.

3. Flip the turkey over, back side down. Now, press the turkey down to flatten it.
4. In a mixing bowl, combine the parsley, rosemary, scallions, thyme, butter, pepper, salt, garlic and onion powder.
5. Rub butter mixture over all sides of the turkey.
6. Preheat your grill to HIGH (450°F) with lid closed for 15 minutes.
7. Place the turkey directly on the grill grate and cook for 30 minutes. Reduce the heat to 300°F and cook for an additional 4 hours, or until the internal temperature of the thickest part of the thigh reaches 165°F.
8. Take out the turkey meat from the grill and let it rest for a few minutes. Cut into sizes and serve.

Nutrition: Calories: 780 Fat: 19g Carbs: 29.7g Protein 116.4g

Hoisin Turkey Wings

Preparation Time: 15 minutes
Cooking Time: 1 hour
Servings: 8

Ingredients:

- 2 pounds turkey wings
- ½ cup hoisin sauce
- 1 tablespoon honey
- 2 teaspoons soy sauce
- 2 garlic cloves (minced)
- 1 teaspoons freshly grated ginger
- 2 teaspoons sesame oil
- 1 teaspoons pepper or to taste
- 1 teaspoons salt or to taste
- ¼ cup pineapple juice
- 1 tablespoon chopped green onions
- 1 tablespoon sesame seeds
- 1 lemon (cut into wedges)

Directions:

1. In a huge container, combine the honey, garlic, ginger, soy, hoisin sauce, sesame oil, pepper and salt. Put all the mixture into a zip lock bag and add the wings. Refrigerate for 2 hours.

2. Remove turkey from the marinade and reserve the marinade. Let the turkey rest for a few minutes, until it is at room temperature.
3. Preheat your grill to 300°F with the lid closed for 15 minutes.
4. Arrange the wings into a grilling basket and place the basket on the grill.
5. Grill for 1 hour or until the internal temperature of the wings reaches 165°F.
6. Meanwhile, pour the reserved marinade into a saucepan over medium-high heat. Stir in the pineapple juice.
7. Wait to boi then reduce heat and simmer for until the sauce thickens.
8. Brush the wings with sauce and cook for 6 minutes more. Remove the wings from heat.
9. Serve and garnish it with green onions, sesame seeds and lemon wedges.

Nutrition: Calories: 115 Fat: 4.8g Carbs: 11.9g Protein 6.8g

PORK

Pork Butt

Servings: 8
Preparation time: 10 minutes
Cooking time: 10 hours and 50 minutes

Ingredients:

- 10 pounds pork butt
- Salt as needed

Directions:

- Open hopper of the smoker, add dry pallets, make sure ash-can is in place, then open the ash damper, power on the smoker and close the ash damper.
- Set the temperature of the smoker to 350 degrees F, let preheat for 30 minutes, then set it to 250 degrees F and continue

- preheating for 20 minutes or until the green light on the dial blinks that indicate smoker has reached to set temperature.
- Meanwhile, score pork butts and then season with salt until well coated.
- Place pork butts on the smoker grill, shut with lid and smoke for 10 hours or until thoroughly cooked and the internal temperature of pork reach to 195 degrees F.
- When done, transfer pork butts to a cutting board, let rest for 10 minutes, then shred with two forks and serve straight away.

Nutrition: Calories: 256; Total Fat: 12 g; Saturated Fat: 4 g; Protein: 32 g; Carbs: 0 g; Fiber: 0 g; Sugar: 0 g

Pineapple Bourbon Glazed Ham

Servings: 8
Preparation time: 10 minutes
Cooking time: 4 hours and 50 minutes

Ingredients:

- 4 pounds spiral cut ham, precooked
- ½ cup ham rub
- 1/2 cup brown sugar
- 1 tablespoon ground mustard
- 1/3 cup molasses
- 1 cup honey
- 18-ounce pineapple preserves
- 1 cup bourbon

Directions:

- Open hopper of the smoker, add dry pallets, make sure ash-can is in place, then open the ash damper, power on the smoker and close the ash damper.
- Set the temperature of the smoker to 350 degrees F, let preheat for 30 minutes, then set it to 225 degrees F and continue preheating for 20 minutes or until the green light on the dial blinks that indicate smoker has reached to set temperature.

- Meanwhile, prepare glaze and for this, place a pot over low heat, add all the ingredients except for ham, whisk well and cook for 20 minutes or until glaze thickens.
- Then remove pot from heat and let the glaze cool until required.
- Take an aluminum foil tray, take a wire rack on top of it, place ham on it and then place on the smoker grill.
- Shut smoker with lid and smoke for 4 hours or until thoroughly cooked, brush with prepared glaze every 15 minutes during the last hour.
- When done, transfer ham to a cutting board, let rest for 15 minutes and then slice to serve.

Nutrition: Calories: 146.3; Total Fat: 0.7 g; Saturated Fat: 0.3 g; Protein: 18 g; Carbs: 15 g; Fiber: 0.6 g; Sugar: 17 g

Pork Tacos

Servings: 6
Preparation time: 25 minutes
Cooking time: 4 hours and 30 minutes

Ingredients:

- 5-pounds country-style pork ribs
- ½ cup all-purpose rub
- ½ cup chopped cilantro
- Chopped mixed greens as needed
- Barbecue sauce as needed
- 6 shell tortillas, soft, warmed
- For Pico De Gallo:
- 1/4 of white onion, peeled and sliced
- 3 Roma tomatoes
- 1 serrano pepper
- ½ teaspoon garlic salt
- 1 lime, juiced

Directions:

- Open hopper of the smoker, add dry pallets, make sure ash-can is in place, then open the ash damper, power on the smoker and close the ash damper.

- Set the temperature of the smoker to 350 degrees F, let preheat for 30 minutes or until the green light on the dial blinks that indicate smoker has reached to set temperature.
- Meanwhile, season pork ribs with the rub until evenly coated on all sides.
- Place pork ribs on the smoker grill, shut with lid and smoke for 3 to 4 hours or until thoroughly cooked and fall part tender.
- In the meantime, prepare Pico De Gallo and for this, place all its ingredients in a bowl and stir until well combined, set aside until required.
- When done, transfer ribs to a cutting board, let rest for 10 minutes and then cut into slices.
- Place pork in warmed taco shells, top with mixed greens and cilantro, drizzle with barbecue sauce and serve.

Nutrition: Calories: 260; Total Fat: 10 g; Saturated Fat: 4 g; Protein: 16 g; Carbs: 28 g; Fiber: 3 g; Sugar: 1 g

Cider Pork Steak

Servings: 4
Preparation time: 2 hours and 40 minutes
Cooking time: 3 hours

Ingredients:

- 4 pork steaks
- 1/3 cup sea salt
- ¼ cup pork rub
- 2 teaspoons dried thyme
- 1 cup maple syrup
- 2 teaspoons hot sauce
- ¼ cup BBQ sauce
- 1½ cup apple cider
- 1½ cup ice water
- 1 cup water

Directions:

- Prepare brine and for this, place a small saucepan over medium heat, pour in 1 cup water, salt, thyme and 1/3 cup maple syrup and cook for 5 to 10 minutes or until salt dissolves completely and brine is hot.
- Then remove pan from the heat, pour in apple cider, 1 teaspoon hot sauce and ice water, stir well until ice dissolves

- and let brine chill for 30 minutes or until temperature of the brine reach to 45 degrees.
- Then place pork steaks in a large plastic bag, pour in brine, seal the bag, turn it upside down to coat steaks with brine and marinate in refrigerator for 2 hours.
- Meanwhile, place remaining maple syrup in a small bowl, add hot sauce and barbecue sauce, whisk until combined and set aside until required.
- When ready to smoke, open hopper of the smoker, add dry pallets, make sure ash-can is in place, then open the ash damper, power on the smoker and close the ash damper.
- Set the temperature of the smoker to 300 degrees F, let preheat for 30 minutes or until the green light on the dial blinks that indicate smoker has reached to set temperature.
- Then remove pork steaks from the brine, pat dry with paper towels, place pork steaks on the smoker grill, shut with lid and smoke for 1 hour 30 minutes to 2 hours or until thoroughly cooked, brushing pork steaks with maple syrup every 3 minutes during the last 10 minutes, flipping steaks halfway through.
- When done, transfer steaks to a cutting board, let rest for 5 minutes and serve straight away.

Nutrition: Calories: 150; Total Fat: 9 g; Saturated Fat: 3 g; Protein: 14 g; Carbs: 3 g; Fiber: 0 g; Sugar: 6 g

Raspberry Chipotle Pork Kebabs

Servings: 8
Preparation time: 10 minutes
Cooking time: 50 minutes

Ingredients:

- 1-pound pork loin, boneless, cut into cubes
- 3 medium green bell peppers, cored and sliced
- 1 large red onion, peeled and cut into cubes
- 2 tablespoons raspberry chipotle spice rub
- 1 tablespoon honey
- 1/8 cup vinegar apple cider
- 1 tablespoon olive oil

Directions:

- Whisk together chipotle seasoning, vinegar, honey and olive oil in a large bowl until combined, then add cubed pork, toss until well coated, then cover the bowl with a plastic wrap and marinate in refrigerator for 1 hour.
- Meanwhile, place eight wooden skewers in a shallow dish, cover with water and let soak for 1 hour.
- When ready to smoke, Open hopper of the smoker, add dry pallets, make sure ash-can is in place, then open the ash damper, power on the smoker and close the ash damper.

- Set the temperature of the smoker to 400 degrees F, let preheat for 30 minutes or until the green light on the dial blinks that indicate smoker has reached to set temperature.
- Meanwhile, remove marinated pork pieces from the marinade and thread evenly in wooden skewers, alternating with onion and pepper pieces.
- Place pork skewers on the smoker grill, shut with lid and smoke for 20 minutes or pork is nicely browned and vegetables are tender, turning halfway through
- Serve straight away.

Nutrition: Calories: 193.2; Total Fat: 10.4 g; Saturated Fat: 3 g; Protein: 15 g; Carbs: 9.4 g; Fiber: 1.4 g; Sugar: 2.5 g

Bacon Cheese Fries

Servings: 2
Preparation time: 10 minutes
Cooking time: 100 minutes

Ingredients:

- ½-pound bacon slices
- 2 large potatoes
- ¼ cup olive oil
- 3 teaspoons minced garlic
- ½ teaspoon salt
- ¼ teaspoon ground black pepper
- 2 sprigs of rosemary
- ½ cup grated mozzarella cheese

Directions:

- Open hopper of the smoker, add dry pallets, make sure ash-can is in place, then open the ash damper, power on the smoker and close the ash damper.
- Set the temperature of the smoker to 375 degrees F, let preheat for 30 minutes or until the green light on the dial blinks that indicate smoker has reached to set temperature.
- Meanwhile, take a large baking sheet, line it with parchment paper and place bacon slices on it in a single layer.

- Place baking sheet on the smoker grill, shut with lid, smoke for 20 minutes, then flip the bacon and continue smoking for 5 minutes or until bacon is crispy.
- When done, transfer bacon to a dish lined with paper towels to soak excess fat, then cut bacon into small pieces and set aside until required.
- Set the temperature of the smoker to 325 degrees F, let preheat for 15 minutes or until the green light on the dial blinks that indicate smoker has reached to set temperature.
- Prepare fries and for this, slice each potato into eight wedges, then spread potato wedges on a rimmed baking sheet in a single layer, drizzle with oil, sprinkle with garlic, salt, black pepper and rosemary and toss until well coat.
- Place baking sheet on the smoker grill, shut with lid, smoke for 20 to 30 minutes or until potatoes are nicely golden brown and tender.
- Then remove baking sheet from the smoker, sprinkle bacon and cheese on top of fries and continue smoking for 1 minute or until cheese melt.
- Serve straight away.

Nutrition: Calories: 388; Total Fat: 22 g; Saturated Fat: 6.8 g; Protein: 9.9 g; Carbs: 38 g; Fiber: 3.5 g; Sugar: 0.5 g

Candied Bacon

Servings: 8
Preparation time: 10 minutes
Cooking time: 2 hours and 30 minutes

Ingredients:

- 1-pound bacon, thick-cut
- 1 cup brown sugar
- 4 tablespoons chipotle spice

Directions:

- Open hopper of the smoker, add dry pallets, make sure ash-can is in place, then open the ash damper, power on the smoker and close the ash damper.
- Set the temperature of the smoker to 200 degrees F, let preheat for 30 minutes or until the green light on the dial blinks that indicate smoker has reached to set temperature.
- Meanwhile, take an aluminum foil tray or a cookie sheet, place a wire rack on it, place bacon slices on the rack and sprinkle its one side with sugar and chipotle spice.
- Place cookie sheet on the smoker grill, shut with lid, smoke for 1 hour, then flip the bacon slices, sprinkle with remaining sugar and chipotle spice and continue smoking for 1 hour until bacon is crispy and nicely browned.
- Serve straight away.

Nutrition: Calories: 77; Total Fat: 4 g; Saturated Fat: 1.4 g; Protein: 4 g; Carbs: 5.2 g; Fiber: 0 g; Sugar: 6 g

Bacon Wrapped Onion Rings

Servings: 8
Preparation time: 10 minutes
Cooking time: 2 hours and 30 minutes

Ingredients:

- 1 pack bacon, thick cut
- 2 white onions

Directions:

- Open hopper of the smoker, add dry pallets, make sure ash-can is in place, then open the ash damper, power on the smoker and close the ash damper.
- Set the temperature of the smoker to 250 degrees F, let preheat for 30 minutes or until the green light on the dial blinks that indicate smoker has reached to set temperature.
- Meanwhile, peel the onions, cut into thirds, separate the onion slices into rings and wrap each onion rings with two bacon slices, securing with a toothpick.
- Prepare more bacon wrapped onion rings until all the bacon is used up.
- Place onion rings on the smoker grill, shut with lid and smoke for 2 hours or until bacon is cooked, turning halfway through.
- Serve straight away.

Nutrition: Calories: 86; Total Fat: 6 g; Saturated Fat: 1.7 g; Protein: 6 g; Carbs: 2 g; Fiber: 0 g; Sugar: 0.4 g

Braised Pork Carnitas

Servings: 6
Preparation time: 15 minutes
Cooking time: 3 hours and 50 minutes

Ingredients:

- 4 pounds pork shoulder, boneless, scored
- 2 teaspoons salt
- 1/2 teaspoon ground cumin
- 2 tablespoons vegetable shortening
- 12 ounces beer
- Water as needed
- For Serving:
- Corn tortillas as required
- Diced onions as needed
- Shredded lettuce
- Sliced radishes
- Fresh cilantro
- Salsa Verde
- Pico de Gallo
- Guacamole

Directions:

- Open hopper of the smoker, add dry pallets, make sure ash-can is in place, then open the ash damper, power on the smoker and close the ash damper.
- Set the temperature of the smoker to 300 degrees F, let preheat for 30 minutes or until the green light on the dial blinks that indicate smoker has reached to set temperature.
- Meanwhile, cut pork into 2-inch pieces, then place in a roasting pan, then pour in beer and enough water to cover the pork pieces and then stir in salt and cumin.
- Place pan on the smoker grill, uncover the pan, shut the smoker with lid and smoke for 3 hours or until pork is tender, stirring occasionally.
- When done, remove the pan from the grill and break the pork into bite-size pieces using a fork.
- Add lard to the pork, then return the pan on the smoker grill and cook for 20 minutes or more until pork is nicely browned.
- Serve pork in corn tortilla along with onion, lettuce, radish, cilantro, salsa, Pico and guacamole.

Nutrition: Calories: 470; Total Fat: 8 1 g; Saturated Fat: 2 g; Protein: 44 g; Carbs: 55 g; Fiber: 8 g; Sugar: 3 g

Cuban Pork

Servings: 10

Preparation time: 20 minutes

Cooking time: 12 hours and 30 minutes

Ingredients:

- 8 pounds pork shoulder, boneless
- 2 medium onions, peeled and cut into rings
- 2 heads of garlic, peeled and chopped
- 3 tablespoons salt
- 1 tablespoon ground black pepper
- 1 tablespoon cumin
- 2 tablespoons oregano
- 4 cups orange juice
- 2 2/3 cups lime juice

Directions:

- Place all the ingredients in a bowl except for salt, black pepper, and pork and stir until well mixed.
- Season pork with salt and black, then place in a large plastic bag, pour in prepared orange juice mixture, seal the bag, turn it upside down and let marinate in the refrigerator for a minimum of 1 hour.

- When ready to smoke, open hopper of the smoker, add dry pallets, make sure ash-can is in place, then open the ash damper, power on the smoker and close the ash damper.
- Set the temperature of the smoker to 205 degrees F, let preheat for 30 minutes or until the green light on the dial blinks that indicate smoker has reached to set temperature.
- Meanwhile, remove pork from marinade, place it in a high sided baking pan and strain marinade on it.
- Place baking pan containing pork on the smoker grill, shut with lid and smoke for 12 hours or until thoroughly cooked and the internal temperature of pork reach to 205 degrees F.
- When done, remove pork from the grill, then shred with two forks, toss until mixed with its liquid and serve.

Nutrition: Calories: 280.1; Total Fat: 9.4 g; Saturated Fat: 3.3 g; Protein: 42.5 g; Carbs: 4.6 g; Fiber: 0.9 g; Sugar: 0.3 g

DESSERT

Bread Pudding

Preparation Time: 15 minutes

Cooking Time: 45 minutes

Servings: 4

Ingredients:

- 8 stale donuts
- 3 eggs
- 1 cup milk
- 1 cup heavy cream
- ½ cup brown sugar
- 1 teaspoon vanilla
- 1 pinch salt
- Blueberry Compote

- 1 pint blueberries
- 2/3 cup granulated sugar
- ¼ cup water
- 1 lemon
- Oat Topping
- 1 cup quick oats
- ½ cup brown sugar
- 1 teaspoon flour
- 2 to 3 tablespoons room temperature butter

Directions:

1. Warmth your Grilla Grill to 350^0.
2. Cut your doughnuts into 6 pieces for every doughnut and put it in a safe spot. Blend your eggs, milk, cream, darker sugar, vanilla, and salt in a bowl until it's everything fused. Spot your doughnuts in a lubed 9 by 13 container at that point pour your custard blend over the doughnuts. Press down on the doughnuts to guarantee they get covered well and absorb the juices.
3. In another bowl, consolidate your oats, dark colored sugar, flour and gradually join the spread with your hand until the blend begins to cluster up like sand. When that is prepared, sprinkle it over the highest point of the bread pudding and toss it on the barbecue around 40 to 45mins until it gets decent and brilliant dark-colored.
4. While the bread pudding is preparing, place your blueberries into a skillet over medium-high warmth and begin to cook them down so the juices begin to stream. When that occurs, include

your sugar and water and blend well. Diminish the warmth to drug low and let it cook down until it begins to thicken up. Right when the blend begins to thicken, pizzazz your lemon and add the get-up-and-go to the blueberry compote and afterward cut your lemon down the middle and squeeze it into the blend. What you're left with is a tasty, splendid compote that is ideal for the sweetness of the bread pudding.

5. Watch out for your bread pudding around the 40 to 50mins mark. The blend will, in any case, shake a piece in the middle however will solidify as it stands once you pull it off. You can pull it early on the off chance that you like your bread pudding more sodden however to me, the ideal bread pudding will be more dim with some caramelization yet will at present have dampness too!

6. Presently this is the point at which I'd snatch an attractive bowl, toss a pleasant aiding of bread pudding in there then top it off with the compote and a stacking scoop of vanilla bean frozen yogurt at that point watch faces light up. In addition to the fact that this is an amazingly beautiful dish, the flavor will take you out. Destined to be an enormous hit in your family unit. Give it a shot and express gratitude toward me.

7. What's more, as usual, ensure you snap a photo of your manifestations and label us in your dishes! We'd love to include your work.

Nutrition: Calories: 290 Carbs: 62g Fat: 4g Protein: 5g

Smoked Chocolate Bacon Pecan Pie

Preparation Time: 1hr 45 minutes

Cooking Time: 45 minutes

Servings: 8

Ingredients:

- 4 eggs
- 1 cup chopped pecans
- 1 tablespoon of vanilla
- ½ cup semi to sweet chocolate chips
- ½ cup dark corn syrup
- ½ cup light corn syrup
- ¾ cup bacon (crumbled)
- ¼ cup bourbon
- 4 tablespoons or ¼ cup of butter
- ½ cup brown sugar
- ½ cup white sugar
- 1 tablespoon cornstarch
- 1 package refrigerated pie dough
- 16 ounces heavy cream
- ¾ cup white sugar
- ¼ cup bacon
- 1 tablespoon vanilla

Directions:

1. Pie:
2. Carry Smoker to 350^0.
3. Blend 4 tablespoons spread, ½ cup darker sugar, and ½ cup white sugar in blending bowl.
4. In a different bowl, blend 4 eggs and 1 tablespoon cornstarch together and add to blender.
5. Include ½ cup dull corn syrup, ½ cup light corn syrup, ¼ cup whiskey, 1 cup slashed walnuts, 1 cup bacon, and 1 tablespoon vanilla to blend.
6. Spot pie batter in 9-inch pie skillet.
7. Daintily flour mixture.
8. Uniformly place ½ cup chocolate contributes pie dish.
9. Take blend into the pie dish.
10. Smoke at 350^0 for 40mins or until the focus is firm.
11. Cool and top with bacon whipped cream.
12. Bacon whipped Cream:
13. Consolidate fixings (16 ounces substantial cream, ¾ cup white sugar, ¼ cup bacon to finely cleaved, and 1 tablespoon vanilla) and mix at rapid until blend thickens. This formula can be separated into 6mins pie container or custard dishes or filled in as one entire pie.

Nutrition: Calories: 200 Carbs: 18g Fat: 0g Protein: 3g

RUBS, SAUCES, MARINADES, AND GLAZES

Smokey Beef Rib Rub

Ingredients:

- 2 Tbsp. brown sugar
- 2 Tbsp. black pepper
- 2 Tbsp. smoked paprika
- 2 Tbsp. chili powder
- 2 tsp onion salt
- 2 tsp garlic powder
- 2 tsp celery salt
- 2 tsp seasoning salt

Directions:

- Mix well and rub both sides of ribs, wrap tightly in plastic wrap, and refrigerate overnight.
- Bring ribs to room temperature before cooking.

Hellfire Cajun Rub

Ingredients:

- 8 Tbsp. smoked paprika
- 4 Tbsp. cayenne powder
- 4 Tbsp. dried parsley
- 4 Tbsp. black pepper
- 2 Tbsp. garlic powder
- 6 Tbsp. fine sea salt
- 2 Tbsp. ground cumin
- 4 Tbsp. dried oregano
- 1 tsp ghost chili powder (to taste)

Directions:

- Combine all the ingredients, mix well and store 24-48 hours, in an airtight container, before using.
- Note: Wear gloves, and use extreme caution, when handling ghost chili powder, even breathing the tiniest amount will be painful.
- This chili has been measured at over 1 million Scoville units (by comparison, Jalapeno peppers are about 4500 Scoville units.)
- This is the hottest Chili Powder available anywhere.
- Start with just a teaspoon…trust me. ;)

Carolina Basting Mop

Ingredients:

- 2 qtrs. Water
- 2 qtrs. Apple Cider Vinegar
- 2 qtrs. vegetable oil
- 1 C liquid smoke
- ½ C salt
- ¼ C cayenne pepper
- ¼ C black pepper
- 1 sweet onion, diced fine

Directions:

- Combine all ingredients and bring to a simmer.
- Allow to cool overnight, and warm before using.
- Use as a rib/chicken baste, or sprinkle on pulled or chopped pork before serving.

Basic Vinegar Mop

Ingredients:

- 2 C cider vinegar
- ½ C vegetable oil
- 5 tsp salt
- 4 tsp red pepper flakes or powder

Directions:

- Combine all ingredients and bring to a simmer, allow to cool overnight to help the flavors marry.
- Keep warm and apply to meat before you close your pellet grill/smoker, when you flip the meat, and again when the meat is done cooking.
- Allow the meat to rest at least 30 minutes to soak up the mop.

- PART 2 -

ELECTRIC SMOKER COOKBOOK

The most notable characteristic of an electric smoker is its shape. Electric smokers all share a unique tall and narrow shape, referred to as a box, cabinet, locker, or block smoker, because of the heat source. Located in the base, the electric heating element radiates heat, which naturally rises to the top of the smoker. Then, as the heat cools slightly, it creates convection. Convection moves heat in waves throughout the insulated box. The insulation in an electric smoker is an important quality, as it directly affects the smoker's ability to contain heat. Although high heat is not associated with smoking, consistent heat is paramount.

APPETIZERS, VEGETABLES, AND SIDES

Smoked Potato Salad

Preparation time: 30 minutes.

Cooking time: 2 hours.

Servings: 4

Ingredients:

- 3 eggs, hard-boiled
- 2 tablespoons cider vinegar
- 1 pound russet potatoes
- 1 tablespoon Dijon mustard
- ½ cup red onion
- 1/3 cup light mayonnaise
- Salt
- Black pepper
- Pickles

Directions:

1. Heat the electric smoker to 225°F.

2. Put prepared wood chips in the wood tray—use mesquite chips for the best result.

3. Put peeled potatoes in a saucepan and cover with water. Put on the lid and bring to a boil.

4. Cook for 20 minutes. Pat potatoes dry, and put them on paper towels.

5. Directly smoke potatoes on the racks for 2 hours as you add extra wood chips in a cycle of 45 minutes.

6. Remove potatoes, let them cool.

7. Chop them well for the preparation of the salad.

8. Combine boiled eggs, onion, mayonnaise, pickles, mustard, pepper, salt, and vinegar.

9. Mix all these ingredients well.

10. Add potatoes to the prepared mixture. Put in the fridge for several hours covered.

Nutrition:

Calories: 209 **Total fat:** 9g **Total carbs:** 30g **Protein:** 3g

Smoked Volcano Potatoes

Preparation time: 15 minutes.

Cooking time: 1 hour.

Servings: 2

Ingredients:

- 2 russet potatoes
- ¾ cup sour cream.
- 1 cup cheddar cheese
- 2 tablespoons green onion
- 8 bacon strips
- 4 tablespoons butter
- 2 tablespoons olive oil
- Salt

Directions:

1. Heat the electric smoker to 250°F.
2. Wash potatoes, pierce using the fork.

3. Take the oil and salt and rub on the potatoes. Wrap the potatoes in foil and put them in the smoker.

4. Smoke potatoes for 3hours.

5. Cut off the top of each potato and remove the potato flesh, leaving the shell empty.

6. Fry and crumble the bacon. Combine potato flesh with bacon, butter, sour cream, and cheese in a bowl.

7. Put the prepared filling in the potatoes, add some cheese on the top.

8. Wrap the potato with 2 bacon slices—for securing, use toothpicks.

9. Smoke for another 1 hour.

10. Add green onions with a little sour cream on top (sour cream will give a special flavor to the potato).

Nutrition:

Calories: 256 **Total fat:** 39.3g **Total carbs**: 31.7g **Protein:** 32.1g

Groovy smoked asparagus

Preparation time: 5 minutes.

Cooking time: 90 minutes.

Servings: 4

Ingredients:

- 1 bunch asparagus
- 2 tablespoons olive oil
- 1 teaspoon chopped garlic
- Kosher salt
- ½ teaspoon black pepper

Directions:

1. Prepare the water pan of your smoker accordingly.
2. Pre-heat your smoker to 275°F/135°C.
3. Fill a medium-sized bowl with water and add 3–4 handfuls of woods and allow them to soak.
4. Add the asparagus to a grill basket in a single layer.

5. Drizzle olive oil on top and sprinkle garlic, pepper, and salt.

6. Toss them well.

7. Put the basket in your smoker.

8. Add a few chips into the loading bay and keep repeating until all of the chips after every 20 minutes.

9. Smoke for 60–90 minutes.

10. Serve and enjoy!

Nutrition:

Calories: 68 **Total fat:** 4.1g **Total carbs:** 7.1g **Protein:** 2.8g

BEEF

Meaty Chuck Short Ribs

Preparation time: 20 minutes.

Cooking time: 5 hours.

Servings: 4

Ingredients:

- 4 tablespoon olive oil

- 4 pounds beef chuck short rib

- 4 tablespoon Pete's western rub

Directions:

1. Remove excess fat on the beef chuck. Drizzle the beef with oil. Season it with Pete's western rub.

2. Heat the Electric Smoker to 275°F. Transfer the rib to the smoker racks.

3. Let it smoke for about 5 hours until the internal temperature reaches 180°F.

4. Let the rib rest for about 20 minutes before serving.

Nutrition:

Calories: 287kcal **Carbs:** 40g **Protein:** 37g **Fat:** 31g

Smoked Pete-zza Meatloaf

Preparation time: 10 minutes.

Cooking time: 8 hours.

Servings: 8

Ingredients:

- 1 cup pizza sauce
- 1 pound ground beef
- 1/2 teaspoon salt
- 1/2 teaspoon garlic powder
- 1 cup bread crumb
- 2 big eggs
- 1/2 teaspoon ground pepper
- 2 tablespoon olive oil
- 3 ounces pepperoni sausage
- 2 cups mozzarella cheese
- 1 cup Portobello mushroom
- 2 cups shredded cheddar

- 2/3 cup green bell pepper
- 1/2 cup red bell pepper
- 2/3 cup red onion, sliced

Directions:

1. In a medium bowl, add the eggs, ground pepper, 1/2 cup of pizza sauce, garlic powder, and salt. Whisk together.

2. Get a skillet, heat the olive oil, fry the red bell pepper, mushroom, green bell pepper, and red onion for about 2minutes. Sprinkle salt and black pepper on the mixture.

3. Get a parchment paper, put the meatloaf on it, then top with pepperoni, place the fried vegetables, and mozzarella. Roll the meatloaf with the parchment paper.

4. Heat the smoker to 275°F. Place the wrapped meatloaf on the smoker rack. Smoke it for about 1hour. Check if the internal temperature is at 180°F.

5. Remove the meatloaf. Let it rest for about 10minutes. Serve it with 1/2 cup of pizza sauce.

Nutrition:

Calories: 345kcal **Carbs:** 31g **Protein:** 48g **Fat:** 36g

Smoked Tenderloin Teriyaki

Preparation time: 30 minutes.

Cooking time: 6 hours.

Servings: 10

Ingredients:

- 4(½) pound (2-kilograms) beef tenderloin

The rub:

- 2 cups brown sugar

- ½ cup Worcestershire sauce

- 3 cups Teriyaki sauce
- 1 teaspoon liquid smoke flavoring
- ½ teaspoon meat tenderizer

Directions:

1. Combine brown sugar with Worcestershire sauce, teriyaki sauce, liquid smoke flavoring, and the meat tenderizer in a bowl. Mix well.

2. Rub the tenderloin with the spice, then marinate overnight.

3. In the morning, remove the spiced tenderloin from the refrigerator, then let it sit for about 30minutes.

4. Heat an electric smoker to 225°F (107°C).

5. Wrap the spiced tenderloin with aluminum foil, then place it in the smoker.

6. Smoke the tenderloin for 6hours and check once every hour. Add soaked hickory wood chips as needed.

7. After 6hours and the internal temperature has reached 165°F (74°C), remove the smoked tenderloin from the smoker, then place it on a flat surface. Let it cool.

8. Once it is cool, cut the smoked tenderloin, then arrange it on a serving dish.

9. Serve and enjoy.

Nutrition:

Calcium: 108mg **Magnesium:** 04mg **Phosphorus:** 668mg **Iron:** 9.24mg **Potassium:** 1098mg **Sodium:** 1815mg **Zinc:** 8.72mg

LAMB

Spicy Brown Smoked Lamb Ribs

Preparation time: 30 minutes.

Cooking time: 4 hours.

Servings: 10

Ingredients:

- 3,5-pound (1.6-kilograms) lamb ribs

The rub:

- ¼ cup brown sugar
- 1 tablespoon Kosher salt
- 1 teaspoon pepper

The sauce:

- 2 cups apricot jam
- 2 tablespoons dried chilies
- 2 tablespoons diced onion
- 1 tablespoon minced garlic
- ¼ teaspoon ground cloves

- ½ teaspoon black peppercorns
- ½ teaspoon ground coriander
- ¾ teaspoon cumin
- 1 teaspoon oregano
- ½ teaspoon Kosher salt
- 3 tablespoons canola oil
- 1 teaspoon ground cinnamon

Directions:

1. Pour water over the dried chilies, then soak for approximately 10 minutes or until softened. Discard the water.

2. Place the softened chilies in a blender, add apricot jam, diced onion, ground cloves, minced garlic, black peppercorns, ground coriander, cumin, oregano, kosher salt, canola oil, and ground cinnamon. Blend until smooth, then set aside.

3. Plug in and turn the Electric Smoker on, then set the temperature to 225°F (107°C).

4. Wait until the Electric Smoker has reached the desired temperature, then add wood chips to the chip tray. Pour apple juice into the water pan.

5. Rub the lamb ribs with brown sugar, kosher salt, and pepper, then place in the Electric Smoker. Smoked the lamb ribs for an hour.

6. After an hour of smoking, take the lamb ribs out of the Electric Smoker and baste apricot sauce over it.

7. Wrap the glazed lamb ribs with aluminum foil, then continue smoking for 3hours or until the internal temperature has reached 63°C

8. Once it is done, remove the smoked lamb ribs from the Electric Smoker and let it rest for approximately 30 minutes.

9. Unwrap the smoked lamb ribs, then transfer them to a serving dish.

10. Serve and enjoy.

Nutrition:

Calcium: 48mg **Magnesium:** 52mg **Phosphorus:** 338mg **Iron:** 3.81mg **Potassium:** 573mg **Sodium:** 319mg **Zinc:** 7.03mg

CHICKEN

Smoked Paprika Chicken

Preparation time: 20 minutes.

Cooking time: 2–4 hours.

Servings: 4

Ingredients:

- 4–6 chicken breast
- 4 tablespoon olive oil
- 2 tablespoon smoked paprika
- ½ a tablespoon kosher salt
- ¼ teaspoon ground black pepper
- 2 teaspoon garlic powder
- 2 teaspoon garlic salt
- 2 teaspoon black pepper
- 1 teaspoon cayenne pepper
- 1 teaspoon rosemary

Directions:

1. Pre-heat your smoker to 220°F using your favorite wood chips.

2. Prepare the chicken breast according to your desired shapes and transfer to a greased baking dish.

3. Take a medium bowl and add spices, stir well.

4. Press the spice mix over the chicken and transfer the chicken to the smoker.

5. Smoke for 1–1 and a ½ hours.

6. Turn-over and cook for 30 minutes more.

7. Once the internal temperature reaches 165°F.

8. Remove from the smoker and cover with foil.

9. Rest for 15 minutes.

10. Enjoy!

Nutrition:

Calories: 237 **Fats:** 6.1g **Carbs:** 14g **Fiber:** 3g

Fully Smoked Herbal Chicken

Preparation time: 10 minutes.

Cooking time: 60 minutes.

Servings: 8

Ingredients:

- 4–6 chicken breast

- 2 tablespoon of olive oil

- Salt as needed

- Freshly ground black pepper

- 1 pack of dry Hidden Valley Ranch dressing (or your preferred one)

- ½ a cup of melted butter

Directions:

1. Pre-heat your smoker to 225°F using hickory wood.

2. Season the chicken with olive oil and season with salt and pepper.

3. Place the in your smoker and smoke for 1 hour.

4. Take a small bowl and add ranch dressing mix and melted butter.

5. After the first 30minutes of cooking, brush the chicken with the ranch mix.

6. Repeat again at the end of the cooking time.

7. Once the internal temperature of the chicken reaches 145°F, they are ready!

Nutrition:

Calories: 209 **Fats:** 13g **Carbs:** 0g **Fiber:** 3g

Orange Crispy Chicken

Preparation time: 8 hours, 30 minutes.

Cooking time: 2 hours

Servings: 4

Ingredients:

For the poultry spice rub:

- 4 teaspoon paprika

- 1 tablespoon chili powder
- 2 teaspoon ground cumin
- 2 teaspoon dried thyme
- 2 teaspoon salt
- 2 teaspoon garlic powder
- 1 teaspoon freshly ground black pepper

For the marinade

- 4 chicken quarters
- 2 cups frozen orange-juice concentrate
- ½ a cup soy sauce
- 1 tablespoon garlic powder

Directions:

1. Take a small bowl and add paprika, chili powder, cumin, salt, thyme, garlic powder, pepper and mix well.
2. Transfer the chicken quarters to a large dish.

3. Take a medium bowl and whisk in orange-juice concentrate, soy sauce, garlic powder, half of the spice-rub mix.

4. Place the marinade over the chicken, then cover.

5. Refrigerate for 8 hours.

6. Pre-heat your smoker to 275°F.

7. Discard the marinade and rub the surface of the chicken with the remaining spice rub.

8. Transfer the chicken to smoker and smoker for 1 and a ½ to 2 hours.

9. Remove the chicken from the smoker and check using a digital temperature that the internal temperature is 160°F.

10. Allow it to rest for 10 minutes.

11. Enjoy!

Nutrition:

Calories: 165 **Fats:** 8g **Carbs:** 14g **Fiber:** 2g

TURKEY

Turkey in the Electric Smoker

Preparation time: 1 hour, 10 minutes.

Cooking time: 10 hours.

Servings: 10

Ingredients:

- 1(10 pounds) whole turkey
- 4 cloves garlic, crushed
- 2 tablespoons salt, seasoned
- ½ cup butter
- 1(12 fluid ounce) cola-flavored carbonated beverage
- 1 apple, quartered
- 1 onion, quartered
- 1 tablespoon garlic powder
- 1 tablespoon salt
- 1 tablespoon black pepper

Directions:

1. Heat the electric smoker to 225°F and then rinse the turkey well underwater, pat dry, and then rub it with seasoned salt.

2. Place it inside a roasting pan.

3. Combine cola, butter, apples, garlic powder, salt, and pepper in a bowl.

4. Fill the cavity of the turkey with cola, apples, garlic powder, salt, and pepper.

5. Rub the butter and crushed garlic outside of the turkey as well.

6. Cover the turkey with foil.

7. Smoke the turkey for 10 hours at 250°F.

8. Once it's done, serve.

Nutrition:

Calories: 907 **Total fat:** 63.2g **Saturated fat:** 22.3g **Cholesterol:** 4256mg **Sodium:** 2364mg **Total carbohydrate:** 17.9g **Dietary fiber:** 1.1g **Total sugars:** 9.7g **Protein:** 62.7g **Calcium:** 462mg **Iron:** 19mg **Potassium:** 710mg

PORK

Smoked Pork Loin with Sweet Habanero Rub

Preparation time: 30 minutes.

Cooking time: 3 hours.

Servings: 8

Ingredients:

- 4 pounds pork loin
- Tamari sauce
- Mandarin habanero seasoning or any other hot sauce
- 1 cup honey
- 1 cup mustard
- 1 tablespoon salt and white pepper to taste

Directions:

1. Combine the Habanero seasoning, honey, mustard and tamari sauce in a mixing bowl.
2. Rub lots of spice mix all over the meat.

3. Heat your electric smoker to 225°F.

4. When it is ready, add some water to the removable pan that is usually on the bottom shelf.

5. Fill the side "drawer" with dry wood chips (hickory or maple).

6. Put meat in the smoker and smoke till the internal temperature is 145°F, about 2(1/2) to 3 hours.

7. When the meat reaches a temperature around 145°F, remove the meat, then cover it for about 5 to 10 minutes.

8. Slice and serve hot.

Nutrition:

Calories: 429,91 **Total fat:** 8,4g **Saturated fat:** 2,78g **Cholesterol:** 149,69mg **Potassium:** 921,88mg **Total carbohydrates:** 36,36g **Fiber:** 0,83g **Sugar:** 34,93g **Protein:** 51,73g

Smoked Pork Ribs with Avocado Oil

Preparation time: 4 hours.

Cooking time: 2 hours.

Servings: 7

Ingredients:

- 1 cup avocado oil
- 1 teaspoon garlic salt, or to taste
- 2 teaspoon garlic and onion powder
- 1/2 cup fresh parsley finely chopped
- 4 pounds spare ribs

Directions:

1. Whisk avocado oil, garlic salt, garlic powder, onion powder, fresh chopped parsley in a mixing bowl.
2. Put pork ribs in a shallow container and pour avocado mixture over; toss to combine well. Refrigerate for at least 4 hours, or overnight.
3. Heat your electric smoker to 225°F.

4. When it is ready, add some water to the removable pan that is usually on the bottom shelf. Fill the side "drawer" with dry wood chips.

5. Remove pork ribs from marinade (reserve marinade) and arrange the pork chops on the rack.

6. Smoke for 1(1/2) hours at 225°F.

7. Remove the ribs, baste generously with reserved marinade, and wrap in heavy-duty aluminum foil.

8. Return the meat to the smoker, then cook for an additional 1 hour, or until internal temp reaches 160°F.

9. Transfer pork chops on serving plate and let rest for 15–20 minutes before serving.

Nutrition:

Calories: 760,68 **Total fat:** 76,26g **Saturated fat:** 21,32g **Cholesterol:** 207,36mg **Sodium:** 505,73mg **Potassium:** 661,57mg **Total carbohydrates:** 1,06g **Fiber:** 0,37g **Sugar:** 0,06g **Protein:** 40,37g

Smoked Pork Ribs with Fresh Herbs

Preparation time: 30 minutes.

Cooking time: 5 hours.

Servings: 6

Ingredients:

- 1/2 cup olive oil
- 1 teaspoon fresh parsley finely chopped
- 1 teaspoon fresh sage finely chopped
- 1 teaspoon fresh rosemary finely chopped
- Salt and ground black pepper to taste
- 3 pound bone-in pork rib roast

Directions:

1. Combine the olive oil, garlic, parsley, sage, rosemary, salt, and pepper in a bowl; stir well.
2. Generously rub the herbs mix all over the meat.
3. Heat your electric smoker to 225°F.

4. When it is ready, add some water to the removable pan that is usually on the bottom shelf.

5. Fill the side "drawer" with dry wood chips (Hickory and mesquite).

6. Smoke the meat directly on the racks for 3 hours at 225°F.

7. Remove the ribs from the racks and tightly wrap them in aluminum foil

8. Move them back in the smoker for 2 hours.

9. Transfer to a serving platter; let it rest 10–15 minutes before serving.

Nutrition:

Calories 532,35 **Total fat** 40,14g **Saturated fat** 7,24g **Potassium** 678,54mg **Total carbohydrates** 0,11g **Fiber** 0,07g **Sugar** 0g **Protein** 40,65g

SEAFOOD

Smoked Tuna

Preparation time: 10 minutes.

Cooking time: 7 hours.

Servings: 4

Ingredients:

- 4 tuna steaks
- 1-gallon water
- 1 cup honey
- ¼ teaspoon garlic, chopped
- 1(1/8) cup sugar
- 1 teaspoon pepper
- 3/8 cup salt

Directions:

1. Add all the ingredients except tuna steaks into the pot and stir well.

2. Add tuna steaks. Cover and place in the refrigerator overnight.

3. Heat the smoker to 140°F/60°C using the applewood chips.

4. Place marinated tuna steaks in the smoker and cook for 7 hours.

5. Serve and enjoy.

Nutrition:

Calories: 700 **Total Fat:** 19.3g **Saturated Fat:** 4.5g
Protein: 8.1g **Carbs:** 133.2g **Fiber:** 0.9g **Sugar:** 125.9g

Smoked Snapper Fillet

Preparation time: 10 minutes.

Cooking time: 60 minutes.

Servings: 6

Ingredients:

- 1(½) pounds red snapper fillets
- 1 tablespoon garlic, granulated
- 3 tablespoon brown sugar
- 2 quarts water
- 1 tablespoon maple syrup
- 1 tablespoon black pepper
- 2 tablespoon olive oil
- Kosher salt

Directions:

1. **For the brine:** Add water, salt, garlic, and 2 tablespoon brown sugar in a pot and stir well.

2. Add fish fillets in brine and set aside for 2 hours.

3. Mix together olive oil, 1 tablespoon brown sugar, and pepper and rub over fish fillets.

4. Heat the smoker to 225°F/107°C using the applewood chips.

5. Place fish fillets in the smoker and cook for 60 minutes.

6. Brush fish fillets with maple syrup and serve.

Nutrition:

Calories: 216 **Total fat:** 6.7g **Saturated fat:** 1.1g
Protein: 30g **Carbs:** 7.8g **Fiber:** 0.3g **Sugar:** 6.4g

Delicious Trout Fillets

Preparation time: 10 minutes.

Cooking time: 3 hours.

Servings: 4

Ingredients:

- 4 trout fillets
- 1 teaspoon lemon pepper
- ¼ cup teriyaki sauce
- ¼ cup soy sauce
- 2 cups of water
- ½ tablespoon salt

Directions:

1. In a bowl, mix together water, soy sauce, teriyaki sauce, and salt.
2. Place fish fillets in a bowl. Cover and place in the refrigerator. Store for overnight.

3. Heat the smoker to 225°F/107°C using the alder wood chips.

4. Place marinated fish fillets in the smoker and cook for 3 hours.

5. Serve and enjoy.

RUBS, SAUCES, MARINADES, AND GLAZES

6-Ingredient Turkey Brine

Preparation time: 5 minutes.

Cooking time: 0 minutes.

Servings: 12

Ingredients:

- 2 gallons water
- 1 ½ cups canning salt
- 1/3 cup brown sugar
- ¼ cup Worcestershire sauce
- 3 tablespoons minced garlic
- 1 tablespoon black pepper

Directions:

1. Mix all the ingredients in a container big enough for your turkey.
2. Soak the turkey in the brine, covered, in the fridge for 1–2 days.
3. Rinse meat before smoking.

Nutrition:

Total fat: 0g **Saturated fat:** 0g **Cholesterol:** 0mg **Sodium:** 11596mg **Total carbohydrate:** 6g **Dietary fiber:** 0.2g **Total sugars:** 4.9g **Protein:** 0.2g

Brine for Fish

Preparation time: 5 minutes.

Cooking time: 0 minutes.

Servings: 8–10

Ingredients:

- 8 cups water
- 2 cups soy sauce
- 1(½) cups brown sugar
- ½ cup kosher salt
- 1(½) tablespoons ground garlic

Directions:

1. Mix all the ingredients.
2. Pour into a bag with the fish, so it's all covered.
3. Marinate for at least 8 hours.
4. Pat fish dry before smoking.

Nutrition:

Total calories: 110 **Protein:** 3.2g **Carbs:** 25.2g **Fat:** 0g **Fiber:** 0.4g

Lightning Source UK Ltd.
Milton Keynes UK
UKHW021841170621
385713UK00002B/363